IMAGES
of America

MESA VERDE
NATIONAL PARK

IMAGES
of America

MESA VERDE
NATIONAL PARK

Duane A. Smith

ARCADIA
PUBLISHING

Published by Arcadia Publishing
Charleston, South Carolina

Printed in the United States of America

Library of Congress Control Number: 2008941498

For all general information contact Arcadia Publishing at:
Telephone 843-853-2070
Fax 843-853-0044
E-mail sales@arcadiapublishing.com
For customer service and orders:
Toll-Free 1-888-313-2665

Visit us on the Internet at www.arcadiapublishing.com

To longtime and dear friends Dianne and Lee Walker

CONTENTS

ACKNOWLEDGMENTS

Mesa Verde has fascinated arrivals to southwestern Colorado for well over 100 years and me for over four decades. It not only has history stretching back several millenniums, it is a beautiful land set in a spectacular region of deserts, mountains, river valleys, plateaus, and sweeping landscapes.

No author writes alone. I owe a deep debt of thanks to longtime friend and collaborator John Ninnemann, who once again took to the field to capture the essence of the story. My appreciation and thanks also go to the very helpful staff of the Mesa Verde Research Center. The staffs of the various museums and archives where the other photographs were found also earn my gratitude.

Three cheers to the helpful and enthusiastic staff of Arcadia Publishing, particularly patient Devon Weston. My wife, Gay, once again uncomplainingly edited and lovingly explained to me why my writing needed to be focused and literate.

The majority of the photographs come from the Mesa Verde National Park archives, and those that do not are so identified.

INTRODUCTION

Mesa Verde National Park, America's first archaeological park and the world's first cultural park, sits in southwestern Colorado's corner, near the only point in the United States where four states meet. Established in 1906, it has now been a magnet attracting tourists, scholars, and archaeologists from throughout the world for over a century.

Settlement in the region, however, dates back 2,200 years, give or take a few decades, or maybe centuries. While Greece and Rome rose and fell, Egyptian dynasties passed into history, Christians and Moslems established their faiths, and European monarchies ebbed and flowed, native peoples, unknown to them all, lived, worked, and died in the caves, mesa tops, and valley floors of this unforgiving land.

Prehistoric Puebloan people, initially the hunters and gatherers, moved in and out of the area before finally settling down to hunt, raise and gather food, and build dwellings and villages. For their part of the world, they were the most advanced culture of their time. In the present United States, they rank at the top, or near the top, of native cultures.

Then, sometime in the late 13th century, they began to depart, leaving behind much that recorded their culture and times. It seemed almost as if they planned to return, but they never did. They simply passed into history. Probably they joined other tribes that lived along the life-sustaining Rio Grande or in the surrounding countryside, where some people already had deep roots.

Why would they leave after all those decades and centuries? The reasons most likely are many, but because they left behind no written records and no one saw them depart to record the moment, we may never know. Having lived and farmed in the area for over a thousand years, they may have found the soil wearing out and their crops declining while their population was growing. Certainly, they traveled farther to find wood to gather and animals to hunt since the local resources must have become exhausted.

There can be no question that the climate had become warmer and drier. No matter what ceremonies they conducted, or prayers they offered, the rains did not come or failed to sustain their crops. A 30-year drought in the late 13th century may have been the final blow, although they had weathered droughts before.

More controversial is the idea that perhaps a civil war broke out. Why did they move into caves, where entry and egress often were so difficult and dangerous? No outside enemy threatened them. Maybe the stresses of urban living proved too much for them.

There are indications of cannibalism. Why? No answer is apparent. The answer might be as simple as having overexploited their environment and exhausted their way of life. All told, it is a mystery, one that has fascinated archaeologists and others for well over 125 years. That is part of the allurement of this fascinating place. Mesa Verde is an enigma wrapped in the eons.

Before they departed for the last time, these people had done some amazing things. Their architecture and buildings alone were accomplishments. Until the multistoried, steel-frame buildings of the 1870s, Cliff Palace contained the tallest man-made structure in the United States.

They undoubtedly understood astronomy and its relation to the seasons. Without domesticated farm animals in an agricultural economy, they survived in a land growing increasingly hostile as the generations slipped away.

They left, and the seasons passed. Not for another century or so would another people arrive. They became known as the Utes. What followed their arrival may be described as the passing of the entire American frontier.

Spanish explorers, priests, and traders appeared in the 17th and 18th centuries. They left behind names, lost mines, and legends, and the first European knowledge of the region. Eventually, following in their footsteps, came the fur trappers. One of them, William Becknell, wintered in the area in 1824–1825. He wrote a letter to his Missouri hometown newspaper about "stone houses and broken pottery."

The land became a section of America in 1848, and government expeditions and military columns soon crisscrossed the region. That same year, the California Gold Rush changed Western history forever. Ten years later, miners scurried to the Pike's Peak country, and, by 1860, they had reached the Animas River at its headwaters in the San Juan Mountains. Little gold and isolation drove them out in 1861.

A decade later, however, back came miners and, this time, settlers too. Parrott City, at the mouth of La Plata Canyon, was less than a long day's trip away, and Mancos would soon be even closer.

By 1874, stories were circulating around Colorado about strange houses and "marvelous cities of the cliffs" in the southwest part of the territory. Interested in this possibility, photographer William Henry Jackson came to Parrott City, from where he was guided into Mancos Canyon. On September 9, 1874, he and the others of his party saw what became known as Two Story House.

The next morning, he took photographs of it and eventually traveled all the way around Mesa Verde without penetrating its forbidding, deep canyons. From Jackson to the Wetherill family and the "discovery" of Mesa Verde, then stretching on to the decade women lobbied for the establishment of a park, is a two-decade journey.

Meanwhile, others came in the 1870s and 1880s to write about and wonder about what they saw. But they did not venture into the future park, with one known exception, who inscribed his name, S. E. Osborn. That was the first, but not the last, mark of someone's passage. Not until a December day in 1888, however, did someone (Richard Wetherill) penetrate Mesa Verde, and he actually took out relics and put them on exhibit for all to see. That discovery of Cliff Palace forever changed Mesa Verde.

Now the pace picked up, with collections taken out, news spread abroad, and the beginning of the struggle to preserve Mesa Verde for posterity. In the end, the women persevered and preserved. They saved Mesa Verde, and the park was established. Tourists started coming in increasing numbers, archaeologists carried on excavations, and the park facilities were slowly developed. After World War II, Mesa Verde came of age as a tourist attraction. Then the question became, would we love it to death?

What follows is a pictorial record of those times and struggles, stretching from the 19th century through the 20th century and into the 21st century. It is a fascinating tale not of Western "daring do," but of the development of a national park against the background of events both within and without of the region.

One

BEFORE THE PARK

Isolated southwestern Colorado and the Four Corners region, where Colorado, New Mexico, Arizona, and Utah meet, has a history of human occupation that stretches back over 2,200 years. During that period of time, prehistoric Puebloan settlement ebbed and flowed until the valleys and mesas were totally abandoned in the late 13th century. Finally, 100 years or so later, the Utes moved into the region.

Starting in the 17th century and throughout the 18th century, Spanish explorers and missionaries probed this fascinating land, and then, in the 19th century, fur trappers wandered about seeking beaver. The Old Spanish Trail, from New Mexico to California, also cut through the land. After the area became American territory in 1848, explorers arrived.

Not until the 1870s, however, did a permanent settlement appear, along with prospectors lured by the hope of finding silver and gold. Plenty of legends of lost mines and buried treasure floated about, whetting the insatiable golden appetite and silver dreams of those early prospectors and miners.

As the prospectors arrived, so did townspeople, ranchers, and farmers to serve the needs of the miners. Little mining camps, such as Parrott City, and small farming communities, like Animas City (the term city always implied more than actually existed!), took root near the mines and in the river valleys.

Settlers encountered plenty of evidence of earlier Puebloan settlement because sites were scattered about hither and yon. The newcomers gathered some collections of pots and whatever else they could find, and the news eventually spread beyond southwestern Colorado. Eventually, people started coming to see the ruins of these ancient peoples.

POINT LOOKOUT. What now is referred to as Point Lookout has been a prominent geographic feature from the days of the Spanish. Soldiers from Fort Lewis, for example, used it to flash heliographic signals to troops campaigning to the west.

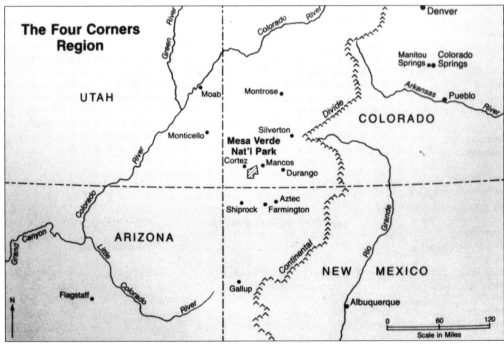

MESA VERDE. Southwestern Colorado was one of the most isolated spots in the state until the railroad arrived in 1881 in Durango. Only a few trappers, soldiers, and explorers had ventured into this terra incognita. (Courtesy of the author.)

WILLIAM HENRY JACKSON. This noted photographer returned to Mesa Verde numerous times after 1874. His photographs helped generate interest in the area and were a factor in creating the national park, just like he had done for Yellowstone.

EARLIEST INSCRIPTION. S. E. Osborn was one of those who ventured into Mesa Verde and left their names to mark their passage. He wrote to a Denver newspaper that he spent "many pleasant days . . . among those ruins." Osborn may have visited Balcony House and Cliff Palace, but no one had named them yet.

TWO STORY HOUSE. Noted photographer William Henry Jackson heard about the mysterious ruins in 1874. Guided by miner John Moss, he traveled down Mancos Canyon and, late in the day, saw Two Story House. Jackson's photographs announced that something fascinating existed here.

CLIFF PALACE. What Osborn saw probably was similar to this photograph of Cliff Palace, taken around 1890. Early visitors had to be careful because rattlesnakes inhabited the sites. Exploding a stick of dynamite scared them back into their holes but did little for the fragile walls and buildings. (Courtesy of Colorado Springs Pioneers Museum.)

Mary Virginia Donaghe.

VIRGINIA DONAGHE. Colorado Springs writer and teacher Virginia Donaghe became fascinated by southwestern Colorado and its mysteries. In the 1880s, she made several visits, saw sites, and developed a lifelong passion about the puzzling ruins. (Courtesy of the author.)

WETHERILL FAMILY. The Wetherills settled in Mancos, a small farming settlement. They became friends of the Southern Utes, who allowed them to winter their cattle in Mancos Canyon. From their neighbors, they heard stories about strange dwellings in Mesa Verde.

UTES. The Utes never went into Mesa Verde. They believed that if you disturbed the spirits of the dead, then you would die too. (Courtesy of Special Collections, Colorado College.)

ANIMAS CITY. Folks in Animas City, Durango, and throughout the Animas Valley, both north and south, were collecting relics for themselves and to sell to tourists years before the Wetherill discovery. (Courtesy of the United States Geological Survey.)

DURANGO, 1890s. The Wetherills took their first collection to Durango, where they made another discovery: that people would pay to see what they had found. Particularly, they paid to see mummies. From Durango, the Wetherills traveled to Denver, where they sold the collection to the State Historical Society. (Courtesy Amon Carter Museum.)

ALAMO RANCH. Word spread quickly about the sites, and the Wetherills' Alamo Ranch became the jumping-off point to visit the intriguing ruins. It took one day by horse from the ranch. Then the visitors could roam about making their own collections.

GUSTAF NORDENSKIOLD. A 22-year-old Swedish tourist and college graduate, Gustaf Nordenskiold heard about Mesa Verde and arrived at the Alamo Ranch in June 1891. No more important visitor ever came to the Wetherills' home.

LITTLE LONG HOUSE. Gustaf Nordenskiold wrote, "My intention was to stay about a week. Now the week has gone, and I have made up my mind to stay for one or two months." Guided by

Richard Wetherill and his brothers Al and John, Nordenskiold visited the sites and collected relics, including from Little Long House.

LONG HOUSE. Nordenskiold ventured everywhere in the future park, numbering, naming, and photographing site after site. His 1893 book, *The Cliff Dwellers of Mesa Verde*, forever solidified his place in archaeology and in the park's history.

BALCONY HOUSE. Nordenskiold took this photograph of Balcony House, which amply displays the condition of the sites in the 1890s. A trained scientist, he worked long hours every day. According to Nordenskiold, starting a 6:00 a.m., "we dig, sketch, photograph, label finds and so on till the sun is high in the sky."

PAINTED KIVA HOUSE. Venturing into sites such as Painted Kiva House was quite an adventure for Nordenskiold and his companions. Nordenskiold confronted skunks, "horrid creatures," and dust, and he "couldn't dig in it for more than 15 or 20 minutes" before needing fresh air, but he continued on with his work.

CAMPING IN MESA VERDE. Camping at the sites with hatless Richard Wetherill and bearded Charlie Mason, Nordenskiold finished his work by September 5th. He then packed his artifacts and took them to Durango to be shipped to Sweden.

DURANGO. Gustaf Nordenskiold suddenly found himself in a peck of trouble as Durango and Denver newspapers accused him of "stealing our heritage." Arrested, Nordenskiold had to retain a lawyer, but there was no law prohibiting acquiring a collection or sending it out of the country, so he went free, and his collection traveled on to Sweden. (Courtesy of the Strater Hotel.)

ALAMO RANCH. The Wetherills spent the better part of the next decade guiding people from their Alamo Ranch into Mesa Verde. As Al Wetherill observed, "the cliff-dwelling work was much more exciting than hunting gold because we never knew what we might find."

WETHERILLS. Richard Wetherill (left) and his family have been both praised and damned for their work at Mesa Verde and elsewhere in the southwest. However, they made several contributions, including calling attention to Mesa Verde and pioneering techniques in excavation work.

WETHERILL MUSEUM. At the Alamo Ranch, visitors could examine the family's "museum" with both natural and archaeological exhibits mixed together. Thanks to the Wetherills, neighboring Mancos was enjoying a tourist boom.

MESA VERDE ACCOMMODATIONS. Rough accommodations greeted tourists as they arrived near Spruce Tree House. From this point, they were either guided to the sites or visited nearby ones on their own, and they toured and collected. As one person later remembered, "We took many artifacts like corn grinders out with us."

KELLY'S CABIN. Charles Kelly, who built this cabin, was the chief rival of the Wetherills in leading visitors into Mesa Verde. Long after the Wetherills left, Kelly was actively involved in the tourist business. (Courtesy of William Winkler.)

WETHERILLS. Al Wetherill (center, back) guided this party. In order to protect the virtue of women visitors, at least two had to be on every trip. If there was not a second female visitor, the group hired a young girl from Mancos as a companion. Every group brought their cameras as Americans fell in love with the new handheld models.

CHICAGO WORLD'S FAIR. It might have been a year late, but America celebrated the 400th anniversary of Christopher Columbus's arrival in 1893. Chicago hosted the event with the World's Columbian Exposition. Among the featured attractions was this reproduction of Battle Rock, which contained a Mesa Verde exhibit. (Courtesy of the author.)

WORLD'S FAIR IN 1893. Inside the Mesa Verde exhibit were Balcony House, Square Tower House, and Cliff Palace modeled at one-tenth of their size. One of the few fair exhibits for which there was an extra charge, it cost 25¢ for admission and 10¢ for a catalog. According to an official guide, at the end of the exhibit sat a museum that included "mummies" placed "so as not to offend those who did not care to look at such things." (Courtesy of Karen and Mark Vendl.)

MANCOS, COLORADO. Mancos found itself a tourist destination and enjoyed a minor boom. The Rio Grande Southern Railroad allowed visitors to arrive in a comfort and ease that was unknown before. Visitors then traveled on by horse.

CORTEZ, COLORADO. There is nothing like a potential tourist bonanza to arouse local urban jealousies. Cortez sat just west of Mesa Verde and dreamed of becoming the gateway to the area. Dream was about all it could do, though, since a visitor had to pass through Mancos to get to Cortez and no railroad reached the small community.

DURANGO, COLORADO. Durango considered itself the gateway to Mesa Verde and got into a nasty little squabble with rival Mancos. The region's largest metropolitan city, in its own eyes, Durango's population topped 3,300 in 1900, leaving Mancos's 383 and Cortez's 125 far behind. (Courtesy of the Colorado Historical Society.)

VIRGINIA MCCLURG. The now married Virginia Donaghe McClurg continued her interest in these ancient people. Visiting Mesa Verde, she realized that it was being vandalized, unintentionally or not, and she and other women set about on a decade-long crusade in the mid-1890s to make the public aware and to create a park in the area. (Courtesy of the Pioneer's Museum, Colorado Springs.)

LUCY PEABODY. Virginia McClurg gained an important ally in politically savvy Lucy Peabody, who joined in trying to persuade Pres. William McKinley and Congress to create a park. They worked diligently and steadily toward their goal but had failed to achieve it as the century turned. (Courtesy of the Colorado Historical Society.)

COLORADO CLIFF DWELLERS ASSOCIATION. These women eventually organized the Colorado Cliff Dwellers Association (with a $2 yearly membership) that had chapters in five states. One of their most active chapters was in Durango, where women like Estelle Camp served as a hostess for visitors and organized trips into Mesa Verde. (Courtesy of the Southwest Center, Fort Lewis College.)

IGNACIO. The women boldly set out to save Mesa Verde. They traveled to Navajo Springs to talk with the Ute leader, Ignacio, about a lease on the Mesa Verde ruins. Ignacio proved too hard of a bargainer, and they failed to reach an agreement at the 1899 meeting. (Courtesy of the author.)

PRIMITIVE CONDITIONS. By the early 20th century, people were visiting Mesa Verde in larger numbers. Unlike their descendents, they struggled over rocks and up and down ladders to get to the sites.

MUMMY LAKE. Many facets of Mesa Verde have always been a mystery, none more so perhaps than Mummy Lake. Seldom does it have water in it, and speculation about its use dates back to the early days. It is one of the minor stops for visitors. (Courtesy of William Winkler.)

RIO GRAND SOUTHERN RAILROAD. As the 19th century came to a close, the scene was set for an increase in visitation to Mesa Verde. Through articles, interviews, and the women's activities, Mesa Verde was becoming better known, and the Rio Grande Southern Railroad made it easier than ever for tourists to visit the area. (Courtesy of the author.)

Two

PARK'S BIRTH
AND EARLY YEARS

It proved quite a struggle for the women and their association to finally convince Congress that Mesa Verde should be a national park. Unfortunately, as they neared victory in 1906, their movement broke asunder over rivalries within the group and jealousy between two towns—Denver and Colorado Springs.

Virginia McClurg, with doubts about Washington, decided that a park controlled by the women would be best and split from the movement. Lucy Peabody and her followers pushed on and won in June 1906, when Pres. Theodore Roosevelt signed the park bill. The distraught McClurg then went to help build her own cliff dwellings at Manitou Springs, Colorado.

Terribly isolated geographically, Mesa Verde's attendance grew slowly. A new entry road was finished in 1913, and the first automobiles chugged and struggled into the park in 1914. Meanwhile, archaeologists arrived, and planned excavations replaced earlier pot-hunting digs. Some of the park rangers, meanwhile, were selling relics on the side.

In the 20th century's first two decades, the park administration was run by political appointees, and, in many cases, professionalism was lacking. Mancos benefited from its nearness to Mesa Verde but still faced rivalry from larger, aggressive Durango. Cortez's high hopes vanished because it was too remote and lacked good roads to any population area.

By 1920, it had become obvious that changes had to be made. The ungainly teenage years were finished.

HENRY TELLER. The women had to convince venerable Colorado senator Henry Teller of the need for the park before vandals and thoughtless pot hunting ruined sites, caused irreparable damage, and lost irreplaceable relics and material. He finally joined the crusade. (Courtesy of Richard Taylor.)

JOHN SHAFROTH. Colorado congressman John Shafroth quickly came to the aid of the women's cause. He also supported a better roads program, something that was almost equally as needed if Mesa Verde were to ever develop into anything beyond a local attraction. (Courtesy of the author.)

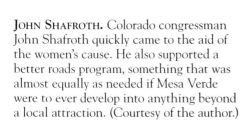

WOMEN. Meantime, the women took matters into their own hands. Estelle Camp and several others traveled to visit with the Ute Mountain Utes to discuss a lease. Their agent and several chieftains agreed and signed. Unfortunately, Washington said no deal. (Courtesy of the Durango Reading Club.)

WOMEN SPLIT. It was at this point that the women began to split, with Virginia McClurg holding out for a women's park, which would allow her maintain her role. She managed to keep control of the Colorado Cliff Dwellers Association in 1906, but it proved a Pyrrhic victory. Undaunted, Lucy Peabody and her Denver/Durango faction kept working with Congress. (Courtesy of William Winkler.)

DURANGO, COLO

UTE RESERVATION. Just as the bill seemed to be making headway, archaeologist Edgar Hewitt pointed out that three of the great cliff houses—Spruce Tree, Balcony House, and Cliff Palace—were not in the park but instead sat on the neighboring Ute reservation. A simple amendment was added to the bill that passed Congress in June 1906.

NATIONAL PARK. The decade-long fight for the park officially ended on June 16, 1906, as shown with "Miss Colorado" presenting Uncle Sam with the cliff dwellings. Mesa Verde was now a national park. (Courtesy of Richard Ballantine.)

CLIFF DWELLINGS

MISS COLORADO: "THEY'LL BE SAFER IN YOUR CARE, UNCLE!"

36

THEODORE ROOSEVELT. An advocate of the strenuous life and outdoors activities, Pres. Theodore Roosevelt signed the bill making Mesa Verde a national park into law. The same month he also signed the Antiquity Act, which provided the first federal protection to "any historic or prehistoric ruin or monument," backed by fines and a possible jail sentence. (Courtesy of Special Collections, Colorado College.)

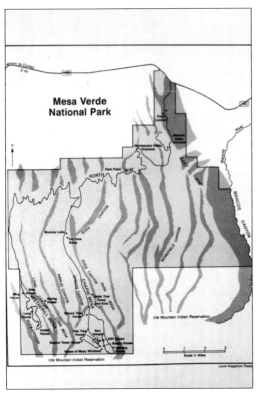

MESA VERDE NATIONAL PARK. Mesa Verde's boundaries have changed only slightly since 1906. The number of open or off-limits sites has changed somewhat, but the visitor from 1906 could easily find her or his way around the park. They would, however, be amazed at the other changes, including the additions of a museum and a restaurant, as well as easy access to sites.

VISITORS. Only 23 visitors arrived the first year and 73 the next. Travel to the new national park still faced the old problems of distance, poor roads, and isolation from any population center. (Courtesy of the La Plata County Historical Society.)

CLIFF PALACE. Early visitors to Mesa Verde saw Cliff Palace as it was just starting to be cleaned up and stabilized. And visitors were still walking off with souvenirs. (Courtesy of the author.)

MANCOS BECOMES HEADQUARTERS. Mancos was now the official park headquarters. The brick and stone two-story building was where the superintendent had his office.

THOMAS RICKNER. Between 1907 and 1913, six superintendents came and went at Mesa Verde; four of them only designated as acting superintendents. Thomas Rickner (right) stopped that trend by serving as superintendent from 1913 into 1921.

JOLLY TOURISTS. A group of tourists gather around a 1910 campfire. Noted archaeologist Alfred Kidder sits in the front row at right. (Courtesy of the Museum of New Mexico.)

PERSONAL COLLECTIONS. Supt. Jesse Nusbaum put a stop to the private collecting of pots and other relics from the park.

JESSE NUSBAUM. Nusbaum had a varied career at Mesa Verde. As a young archaeologist, he excavated and stabilized Balcony House. It became one of the most popular, adventure-filled sites to visit. He is pictured here with his son, Deric, and his wife, Aileen.

BALCONY HOUSE. Balcony House might have been popular, but it was a trial getting there. An earlier visitor recounted going down by rope above a several hundred-foot drop. "Nearly everyone hesitates—the guides encourage us."

SUN TEMPLE. It took a vivid imagination to see this as anything but rubble and a pile of rocks, but this is what Sun Temple looked like before it was excavated and restored.

FAR VIEW HOUSE. Archaeologists were excavating some of the mesa top sites, including Far View House. Jesse Fewkes, who took this photograph, was in charge of the work.

ARCHAEOLOGICAL METHODS. With mules, blows, shovels, picks, and trowels, welcome to archaeology 1916-style. Jesse Fewkes and his crew pose for a moment while excavating Far View House.

FAR VIEW HOUSE, TOO. Visitors finally were getting to see a better picture of the Puebloans life and times when excavation, and in a sense reconstruction, of sites such as Far View House were completed. (Courtesy of Colorado Historical Society.)

SQUARE TOWER HOUSE. In these early days, some sites were open to visitors that would later be closed. Square Tower House took a bit of a walk or ride to get to it, but other places could be visited or closely seen on the way.

CEDAR TREE TOWER. One of the many mysteries that early archaeologists pondered was what use did the ancient people make of structures such as this tower. Were they signal points, watchtowers, or something else?

KIVA. At this unnamed site, a crew stabilizes a kiva and a collapsing wall. Visitors were particularly interested in kivas and their functions in Mesa Verde life. Interpretations about their role have changed over the years, including worship and living purposes.

STABILIZATION. The methods seem primitive today, but with fragile structures in danger of collapsing, stabilization had to be carried out. The ropes leading into Balcony House can be seen in the background. (Courtesy of the Colorado Historical Society.)

TOURISTS AT BALCONY HOUSE. Balcony House was a wonderful site to see when one overcame the fear of actually getting there. A teacher and Durango superintendent of schools, Emory Smiley leads this group to Balcony House. (Courtesy of the La Plata County Historical Society.)

LISLE UPDIKE. Mesa Verde has fascinated both professional and amateur photographers over the years. Durango photographer Lisle Updike faced the challenges of getting to Balcony House to take this photograph. (Courtesy of Jackson Clark.)

FIRST ON A WAGON. This patriotic group was the first to come into the park on a wagon. The road on top of the mesa had never been a problem, but reaching it had meant coming in from the south. Now a road off the Mancos to Cortez highway solved the problem by shortening the trip from the north.

AUTOMOBILES SNEAK IN. Within a year, the first automobiles chugged into the park in early 1914, sneaking ahead of the official opening in June. The trip into the park had been reduced from a day to hours from Mancos. Livery stable owners protested, but there was little they could do; their days were nearly over.

AUTOMOBILES. Just to reach the park from Durango was an exciting adventure in one of the newfangled machines. Gas stations were few, flat tires many, and the road dusty on dry days and muddy, with mud-holes hazards, on rainy days. (Courtesy of the La Plata County Historical Society.)

TOURISTS AND STYLES. As the Victorian era slipped into the Edwardian era, ladies' styles changed, but men's stayed almost the same. This couple is about to board the Rio Grande Southern Railroad in Durango for a trip to Mancos as the country slips toward World War I. (Courtesy of the La Plata County Historical Society.)

WILLA CATHER. The famous author appeared in Mancos and the park in 1915. She decided to stay a few extra days at Mancos. Out of her experiences came one of her lesser-known novels, *The Professor's House.* (Courtesy of Helen Cather Southwick.)

Virginia McClurg. McClurg was not finished with "her" park. In September 1917, she and the Colorado Cliff Dwellers Association staged a last hurrah with a pageant, *The Marriage of the Dawn and the Moon*. Afterward the guests went to a dinner supposedly similar to what the Mesa Verde people would have enjoyed. (Courtesy of the Colorado Historical Society.)

Cars and Trains. To ease the strain on the cars and speed up their arrival, a group of visitors going to see the pageant had their automobiles loaded onto flatcars and transported to Mancos.

Uniformed Women. Patriotism was rampant in the World War I era. This unidentified group of uniformed women was camping out and possibly holding a meeting at the park. (Courtesy of the Western History Department, Denver Public Library.)

ONLY YESTERDAY. It seems like only yesterday when Mesa Verde looked like this. To arrive there was quite an adventure, either as part of a private tour or on one's own to see it.

MESA VERDE, 1919. As the 1920s dawned, many of the sites had been stabilized and opened to the public. Cliff Palace was a favorite site, and one could hardly go home without taking a photograph of it. Tourists were already arriving from far-away places. (Courtesy of Jackson Thode.)

OLDSMOBILE. America's love affair with the automobile was in full swing as the 1910s became the 1920s. In their "merry Oldsmobile," these folks had bumped and struggled over questionable roads all the way from Denver, a major trip in those days. (Courtesy of William Winkler.)

Three

ROARING DAYS AND
DEPRESSION DAYS

World War I was over, as was the reform Progressive Era, and many Americans determinedly decided to let their hair down. The result produced the Roaring Twenties with flappers, bootleg whiskey, radios, big-time sports, fast cars, changing roles for women, and movies that shocked many conservative Americans.

It was not that way in rural southwestern Colorado, however. Mining and agriculture slipped into the doldrums, and population growth slowed. But the region did have Mesa Verde National Park, and tourists were coming in greater numbers. Americans now owned more automobiles than ever before and traveled over better roads to get to Mesa Verde, although it still could be an adventuresome trip. The year 1916, meanwhile, had changed the park forever with the completion of a highway connecting eastern and western Colorado over Wolf Creek Pass and the creation of the National Park Service.

Another major change for the park came when Supt. Jesse Nusbaum moved the park headquarters out of Mancos and into Mesa Verde. Mancos never recovered because visitors bypassed it to stay in the park or in larger Durango, which had more hotels and a variety of things to do. Nusbaum and the National Park Service also brought some much-needed professionalism to Mesa Verde; the days of political appointments ended. The latter came just in time, when visitation increased steadily during the decade, nearly reaching 28,000 in 1928. Visitors came only during the spring, summer, and early fall because Mesa Verde continued to close in the winter.

The 1930s, however, told a different story. Except for the year 1931, visitation in the park dropped during the Depression until 1934, when it picked up again and reached a high of 32,000 visitors by the time the decade ended. But the story of the 1930s was Franklin Roosevelt's New Deal and, particularly for the park, the Civilian Conservation Corps, which sent young men into parks throughout the country to work on a wide variety of projects.

SPRUCE TREE HOUSE. Stabilized and cleaned up, Spruce Tree House, next to the park headquarters (now on Chapin Mesa), remained the most popular visiting spot. Nusbaum was appalled at what some of the earlier guides had told visitors (such as wild stories about giants) and saw to it that the story now reflected the latest archaeological interpretation. (Courtesy of Jackson Thode.)

JOHN D. ROCKEFELLER JR. One of the first things that Jesse Nusbaum did was to improve the museum and its collections. An expert fund-raiser, Nusbaum eventually found a patron in John D. Rockefeller Jr. (left), who helped underwrite the construction of the building that was designed by Nusbaum. (Courtesy of the Western History Department, Denver Public Library.)

SUPERINTENDENT'S HOME. Jesse Nusbaum did more than build a museum; he also designed and helped construct a superintendent's home in an early modified pueblo style in 1921. Unfortunately, some tourists looked upon this as part of their visiting experience, something the National Park Service soon stopped. (Courtesy of John Ninnemann.)

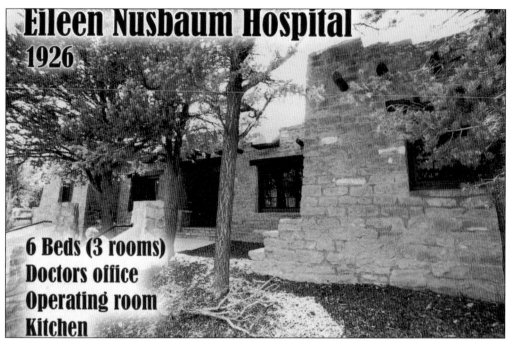

Eileen Nusbaum Hospital
1926

6 Beds (3 rooms)
Doctors office
Operating room
Kitchen

HOSPITAL. Injuries and illnesses plagued some visitors, and Mesa Verde had no facilities to treat them. Jesse Nusbaum and his wife, Aileen, who actually started a tent hospital, finally convinced Congress more was needed. In 1926, the Aileen Nusbaum Hospital, with six beds, a doctor's office, and an operating room, opened. (Courtesy of William Winkler.)

KNIFE EDGE. In 1923, the infamous Knife Edge Road was finished around the west side of Point Lookout. Less steep and shorter than the original road, it pleased Jesse Nusbaum, but few flatlanders drove it. It scared them to death, particularly when some cars had to back up because of traction or half-filled gravity-feed gas tanks in the rear of the car.

AUTO TRIBULATIONS. A thousand-foot, or so, slide awaited the driver if he or she slipped off the Knife Edge Road. Fortunately, "Old Dobbin" is coming to the rescue, and hopefully the driver eventually reached the valley floor safely.

RANGERS. Rangers conducted automobile caravans that started from the museum in the morning and afternoon. With roads now leading out of Chapin Mesa to Balcony House, Cliff Palace, and later the mesa-top structures, the visitors' experience was changing.

INSPECTION. This unidentified group seems to be inspecting an archaeological site. In the 1920s, consideration was given to opening various ruins, but expenses and too few park personnel curtailed the idea. (Courtesy of William Winkler.)

TOUR GROUP. This unidentified photograph obviously shows a tour of park service administrators and employees. Some seem a little concerned about the downward drop.

JESSE NUSBAUM. Nusbaum did more than manage, raise funds, and supervise the park. During the winter, he conducted excavations such as this one in 1926 at Step Cave. Nusbaum is at the right and his son Deric is standing in front of the tent. Deric, with his mother's help, wrote a children's book about the park.

SPRUCE TREE CAMP. A group of seasonal employees are out for a spin. Mesa Verde was a prime summer employer, particularly of college students and younger Americans. (Courtesy of William Winkler.)

ENTRANCE. There was nothing particularly fancy about the entrance to the park in the early 1920s; tourists gathered information, received their permit, and registered. They were also advised that road construction was going on, with the park stating, "We are Building You a Better Park."

TOURIST PHOTOGRAPHS. Hardly a tourist did not want a photograph of his family, himself or herself, or friends taken somewhere in the park. Men still dressed in a tie and white shirt as the 1920s moved along. (Courtesy of the Western History Collections, University of Colorado.)

AUTO TOUR. In the 1920s, ranger-led auto tours became popular. With one in the morning and one in the afternoon, these tours took visitors to some of the important sites and views. It also helped keep the crowds manageable.

Gov. Clarence Morley. In the mid-1920s, Colorado was a Ku Klux Klan–dominated state, and the KKK elected Gov. Clarence Morley and U.S. senator Rice Means into office. The group tried to have a Klan initiation in the park, but Jesse Nusbaum would have none of it. He threatened to arm his workers and rangers with ax handles and drive the Klan out. (Courtesy of Colorado Historical Society.)

GAS STATION. Gas stations now appeared in all the nearby communities and along roads on the way to Mesa Verde. None probably proved more exotic than this one in Durango. (Courtesy of Catherine Conrad.)

5388. Ancient Cliff Dwellings in Phantom Cliff Canon, Colorado, as seen from Manitou Skyline Drive.

MANITOU SPRINGS. Nothing has given Mesa Verde more trouble over the years than the bogus Manitou Springs "cliff dwellings." A bitter Virginia McClurg was partly responsible because she lent her name to the project after the park's creation. Over the years, Manitou tried to discourage visitors from the "long, difficult travel" to Mesa Verde. Manitou Springs was "better!" (Courtesy of the author.)

Navajo Laborers. In the 1920s and 1930s, Navajo laborers were employed in the park and also participated in the evening campfire talks with dances and singing. Some brought their families with them.

HOGANS. These early Navajo hogans, dwellings made of mud and logs, at Mesa Verde were government built. Jesse Nusbaum hoped this would ease the cultural shock for his workers as they moved beyond the reservation into the white man's world. (Courtesy of William Winkler.)

WEAVER. Thanks to the Mesa Verde Company, Navajo women in the 1930s, and later, wove rugs while tourists watched. These demonstrations added a further dimension to the park visit, and many rugs graced visitors' homes. (Courtesy of William Winkler.)

DIORAMA. These dioramas, when completed, became visitor favorites. This one displays the Basket Maker period, roughly from 1 to 450 AD. Basket Maker sites are found throughout the Four Corners region as well as within the park.

CIVILIAN CONSERVATION CORPS. The CCC was created to get unemployed young men (aged 18 to 25) into a military-style camp and put them to work on useful projects. The CCC workers learned a skill, received medical and dental care, and had the opportunity to finish high school.

ROCK QUARRY. Coyne Thompson looked back over his CCC experience and remembered rocks. "We built this big, huge rock fireplace. They didn't have anything for us to do at first so we gathered rocks and built this fireplace," said Thompson.

CONSTRUCTION CREW. "The fellows did trail work, road work and I dug an earth lodge with a bunch of CCC boys," remembered Al Lancaster, who worked for more than 30 years on park projects. "A few were local boys; most of them came from Oklahoma or down in that country."

PRATER CAMP. The initial CCC camp was soon abandoned for two more permanent ones on Chapin Mesa, near the park headquarters. Some of the CCC buildings are still being used as offices and for other functions.

MESS CLEANUP. Robert Beers clearly remembered that the food "was passable." For cleanup, "they had a couple of big sort of tubs with boiling water and you went to the first one and scraped off anything you didn't eat." In the next tub, which "smelled like lye," the dishes were washed.

VOLLEYBALL. "I enjoyed Mesa Verde," recalled John McNamara. Times were hard, and "I was tickled to get in there." The day started at 6:00 a.m. "We had a bugler and after that you had to answer roll call." There was time for recreation in the late afternoon and evening. There were also teams that played local schools.

RECREATION HALL. "At the end of the day, you'd get cleaned up for chow in the evening and then the time was yours, until time to go to bed," said Mesa Verde CCC worker Coyne Thompson.

GAS STATION. Mesa Verde's gas station was not as exotic as the one in Durango, shown earlier. It did provide services that were needed, however, including changing tires and servicing government vehicles.

HEADQUARTERS. By the 1930s, the little village at the end of Chapin Mesa had taken on the form it is today. Jesse Nusbaum's architectural style prevailed.

AMERICAN LEGION PARADE. It is 1933, and the Mesa Verde float is getting ready to join the Durango American Legion Parade. In August 1933, both the park and the community needed the boost tourists brought. The Depression had settled in, and times were not good.

CAMPFIRE TALKS. Jesse Fewkes initiated the campfire talks on an irregular basis in the 1910s, but they became a regular feature soon thereafter. The topic varied each evening, and almost all the rangers gave talks. (Courtesy of William Winkler.)

STAFF, 1933. Mesa Verde's rangers stand proudly for a photograph. Kenny Ross remembered the park in the 1930s: "The experience was to see the lights go on all over the country [REA program]. Driving back and forth, it was very striking. The country was moving out of the real pioneering life into the modern era."

Four

FROM WAR TO
CROWDED DAYS

America entered World War II after the December 7, 1941, attack on Pearl Harbor. Instantly gas rationing, wartime pressures, and young people leaving for the military cut visitation to Mesa Verde. The 4,600-visitor total of 1943 represented the lowest in the past 20 years.

Nor was it much better in the park. Employees volunteered for service or were drafted, park funds were cut, and the CCC camps closed. Rangers conducted only two ruins trips per day. Even the old warhorse, Jesse Nusbaum, returned for one last time as acting superintendent during the war years.

The arrival of peace lured tourists back, and the numbers kept increasing year after year. By 1952, visitation topped 100,000 for the first time and then reached the 600,000 range 20 years later. Congestion, traffic, and mounting threats to the fragile dwellings and the environment gave proof that Mesa Verde was nearly being loved to death. Government expenditures did not allow the park to keep up with necessary improvements, and the park was barely able to maintain itself.

Better roads, increased promotion, newer cars, and even the mounting use of airplane travel carried tourists to southwestern Colorado in ever-increasing numbers. Often they continued the trip throughout the entire Four Corner states to see a variety of national parks and monuments. At last, Cortez finally saw its decades-old gateway realized when an interstate highway connected it with southern California and Arizona.

To try and spread the visitors out a bit and offer a different experience, the Wetherill Mesa was opened, with all of its mesa top and cliff dwelling sites. All told, Mesa Verde National Park would never be the same again.

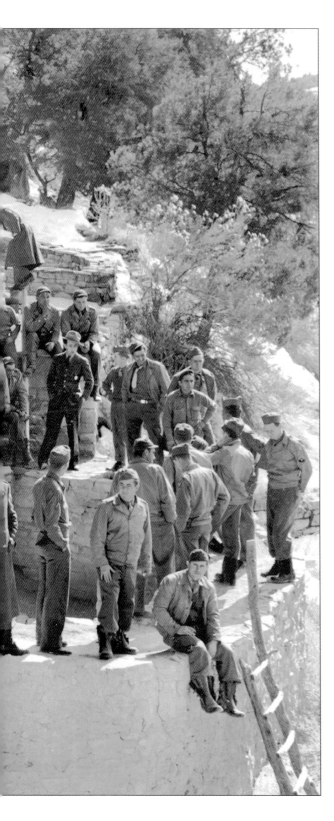

SOLDIERS FROM FORT CARSON.
Soldiers from Colorado Spring's Fort Carson visit the park in 1943. On this day, they outnumbered the few civilians who arrived. Rangers were not overwhelmed with visitors at this time as they would be after 1945.

79

World War II Years. It almost looks as if the troops had arrived for maneuvers. For whatever reason, the park must have been a temporary diversion to take their minds off the more serious problems at hand.

Boy Scouts. This Japanese American Boy Scout troop came from the Granada Internment Camp located in southeastern Colorado. After Pearl Harbor, Japanese were removed from the West Coast and put into internment camps in the interior of the United States.

Summer 1944
Ansel Hall Family on porch of Spruce Tree Lodge

left to right: Roger,Robin,Sylvia, Merrie, June, Laurel & Ansel

ANSEL HALL. During the lean wartime days, Ansel Hall continued to operate his lodge and restaurant, and stayed active to serve the tourists. Pictured here are Ansel (far right); his wife, June (third from right), and their five children. (Courtesy of William Winkler.)

FIRE SCHOOL. The threat of fire always hung over isolated and often dry Mesa Verde. This group of confident young men seemed ready to tackle the problem. They had just finished attending the Mesa Verde Fire School in 1948. (Courtesy of William Winkler.)

ACCOMMODATIONS. Accommodations during the Hall and Winkler years at the Mesa Verde Company steadily improved. They were a far cry from what visitors endured in the early park days. (Courtesy of William Winkler.)

TENTS. Visitors could still "rough it" in tent cabins during the 1950s. There were a variety of tents to chose from and were probably enjoyed most of all by the kids. (Courtesy of William Winkler.)

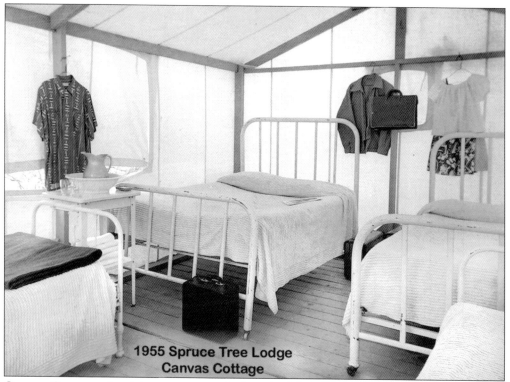

1955 Spruce Tree Lodge
Canvas Cottage

CANVAS COTTAGE. It might appear sparsely furnished, but for the tourist on vacation it was a home away from home. The cottages provided a chance to see Mesa Verde at less expense to the visitor. (Courtesy of William Winkler.)

LUNCH. It must be noontime at the crowded lunch counter as hungry tourists are placing their orders. It was essential to provide food services; the nearest restaurants were an hour or so away. (Courtesy of William Winkler.)

Honeymoon Cabin. The Honeymoon Cabin offered the visitor a wonderful view of Mesa Verde's country and canyons. Looking at this scenery, one can understand why it took so long to discover the cliff dwellings. (Courtesy of William Winkler.)

ANSEL ADAMS. Longtime friends Ansel Hall (right) and Ansel Adams (left) seem to be enjoying a good story. Through photographs and involvement with the parks, they did much to arouse interest in the West. (Courtesy of William Winkler.)

Air Travel. Frontier Airline hostesses check into Spruce Tree Lodge to enjoy a visit at the park. By the 1950s, air travel was becoming more popular, and Frontier helped out by promoting Mesa Verde. Note the poster. (Courtesy of William Winkler.)

Tourism. Spruce Tree Lodge is pictured here on a quiet day in the 1950s. With the restaurant, cabins, and tourist shops crowded together, along with the park headquarters and staff and workers' housing, Chapin Mesa continued to be a congested area. Talks were already underway about changes. (Courtesy of William Winkler.)

FAIR VIEW LODGE. The result of those discussions was the construction of the Far View Lodge and Morefield campgrounds by the Mesa Verde Company. By 1970, eating and sleeping facilities had been moved, and Spruce Tree Lodge belonged to history. (Courtesy of John Ninnemann.)

NAVAJO WOMEN. Navajo women and others from nearby tribes worked in a variety of jobs in the postwar years. The park, meanwhile, was reaching out to nearby tribes for help in interpretation of the sites and work in the park. (Courtesy of William Winkler.)

FAR VIEW LODGE. The new Far View cabins and lodge are seen in the background as a group of tourists departs from one of the company's buses. Guided tours, such as this, were popular after the war. (Courtesy of William Winkler.)

FAR VIEW CENTER. Not only would the lodge be moved, but a new visitor's center was located across the highway. Here visitors could gather information and eventually, as crowds increased, purchase tickets to tour popular Balcony House and Cliff Palace.

SPRUCE TREE TERRACE. The closing of the Spruce Tree Lodge and restaurant, however, created a problem. In order to purchase a meal, one had to travel 12 miles round-trip to Far View. As a result, the old first aid station/hospital was renovated and became Spruce Tree Terrace with souvenirs and food available. (Courtesy of John Ninnemann.)

MOREFIELD. The Morefield campground served the increasing number of people who camped out. Campers had 512 sites to select from, plus an evening campfire talk in the amphitheater, and, among other things, a store and car wash. The popular campfire talks were transferred down here from the Chapin Mesa. (Courtesy of William Winkler.)

MOREFIELD CAMPGROUND. With its gas station, campground, store, and other amenities, Morefield campground became a popular spot in the summer. In fact, on busy days, it was the second-largest community in Montezuma County. (Courtesy of William Winkler.)

MUG HOUSE. September 1958 found national park and National Geographic Society folks examining Mug House, which was named after an exceptional mug found on the site. Over the decades, the society has published numerous articles on Mesa Verde.

CHAPIN MESA OVERCROWDING. The Wetherill Mesa Project was designed with two goals in mind—research and new exhibits. It would also hopefully alleviate overcrowding on Chapin Mesa. Starting in the late 1950s, studies and excavations with modern scientific methods and research techniques spearheaded the project that continued into 1965.

MUG HOUSE SANDSTONE. Among the interesting developments that came out of the Wetherill Mesa Project was the hiring of a miner to build cribbing and then blast down a large sandstone slab threatening Mug House. (Courtesy of Richard Ellis.)

WETHERILL MESA PROJECT.
This wide-ranging project included mesa-top sites. Work was slow, but each year more was learned about the prehistoric people who once lived here.

RELICS. It is amazing how much can still be found at Mesa Verde after all these years. This shows just a portion of what the Wetherill Mesa Project uncovered, a project that expanded the knowledge of the life and times of the inhabitants.

TRAIL RIDES. Once a popular feature in the park, trail rides are now a memory of days gone by. Some of the "dudes" ended up saddle sore; others became scared before reaching "home." (Courtesy of William Winkler.)

MESA VERDE TOUR BUS. For those not wanting to drive or replay the "old West," the Mesa Verde Tours bus proved the perfect answer. Two trips per day brought visitors into the park. (Courtesy of William Winkler.)

WOMEN'S PROGRESS. Supt. Chester Thomas presents Jean Pinkley with her 20-year national park pin. Despite women having saved and created the park, it would be decades before they would have professional jobs at Mesa Verde. For example, not until the 1970s would they be hired as rangers.

NUSBAUM'S LEGACY. Jesse Nusbaum's legacy is seen throughout Mesa Verde, from professionalism to interpretation. Certainly, however, the development of the area's predominant architectural style is one of his outstanding contributions. (Courtesy of John Ninnemann.)

WINTER IN MESA VERDE. Not until 1965 would Mesa Verde maintain a formal winter schedule. Two tours a day brought in 201 people in 1965. The potential popularity of winter was demonstrated the next year when nearly 2,500 people arrived. (Courtesy of Richard Gilbert.)

WINTER'S BEAUTY. Winter is a beautiful time in the park. Only the headquarters and Spruce Tree House were open initially for the formal winter schedule. Now the National Park Service had to keep the roads plowed for tourists, as well as staff. (Courtesy of Richard Gilbert.)

KNIFE EDGE ROAD. The Knife Edge Road, described as "the hair-raising [road] so notorious among tourists," was finally abandoned in 1957. All that remains is a historic marker as the deserted roadbed continues to slide down the side of the mesa. (Courtesy of the author.)

KIDS KORRAL. Mesa Verde is not the best "treat" for little ones, as parents quickly found out, so the Mesa Verde Company opened the popular Kids Korral to entertain them. Toys, playground equipment, and games were featured. (Courtesy of William Winkler.)

SOUVENIRS. Hardly any family could bypass the gift shop with its appealing selection of gifts for all ages and pocket books. Native American products came to be featured as the years went by. (Courtesy of William Winkler.)

BALCONY HOUSE. The Balcony House tour was not for the obese or the faint of heart. Climbing through a keyhole door bedeviled the former, and this ladder scared the latter. Despite ample warnings, some people dared the adventure and found themselves in trouble.

SQUARE TOWER HOUSE. While one could not visit Square Tower House, it was one of the attractions that could be seen from the canyon top. A hurried visitor could go to the museum, hasten to Spruce Tree House, drive the circle road, and be out of the park in half a day. (Courtesy of Richard Gilbert.)

STABILIZATION CREW. Every since the park was created, stabilization crews have been battling both Father Time and increasing visitation. Seldom interfering with the visitor's tour, they are essential to having a rewarding visit.

Mesa Verde. The beauty of Mesa Verde National Park—its canyons, mesas, and panoramas—adds to the visitors' appreciation of the southwest. (Courtesy of John Ninnemann.)

Mesa Verde Museum. Mesa Verde's museum has always been a popular spot. Slowly the National Park Service recovered items from archaeological excavations, as well as relics that had "wandered from the park" and came home to be exhibited. (Courtesy of Richard Gilbert.)

CHANGING STYLES. As the 1980s passed into history, tourists kept coming and venturing into kivas. Their clothing styles had changed over the past decades, however. (Courtesy of William Winkler.)

SHUTTLE TRAMS. Shuttle trams carried visitors around Wetherill Mesa, but even this added convenience did not entice people to leave the "tried and true" sites for the new ones. (Courtesy of William Winkler.)

PARK RESIDENCE. The long drive to the nearest town produced the need to have homes on Chapin Mesa for some of the park staff. The Nusbaum architectural style was maintained with these buildings. (Courtesy of William Winkler.)

Five

INTO A NEW MILLENNIUM AND CENTURY

As the 20th century raced toward becoming the 21st century, Mesa Verde's life and times changed almost as rapidly. At least 12 percent of the visitors came from foreign counties by the mid-1980s. As a World Heritage Cultural Site, Mesa Verde's visitation had become truly global. The park now distributed handouts in five languages but found it hard to locate and hire bilingual rangers.

Those longtime, never-ending issues—stabilization and maintenance—continued to roll on year after year, and a new issue arose in more magnitude than earlier—air quality. Not just for the quality of the visitors' experience, but the question of pollution's effect on the cliff dwellings and mesa-top sites. Then major fires in the 1990s and early in the new millennium, especially in 2002, burned over nearly three-quarters of the parkland. It is expected to take generations before the vegetation will be totally restored.

One thing the fires did was to uncover even more sites than had been thought to exist. This was both a positive and, in some ways, a negative, as there were now more locations to be concerned about.

The park's continuing popularity also caused problems. While fluctuating tourist numbers remained in the 500,000 to 600,000 range, with occasional years topping 700,000, the rising cost of gasoline and travel in general raised questions about the future. All this happened as the National Park Service continued forward with its original congressional charge to preserve and protect the sites and artifacts of the ancestral Puebloan people.

All was not gloom and doom, though. With appropriate ceremonies, Mesa Verde National Park celebrated its centennial in June 2006. Now, as it moves into its second century, Mesa Verde faces old problems and new as the National Park Service plans for an exciting, challenging future.

RANGERS AND TOURISTS. As the century turned, tickets were needed, and had to be purchased, to visit Balcony House and Cliff Palace. Rangers in the three main sites were there to lecture and answer questions for the crowds of people swarming about. These tourists are studying their choices.

RANGER AT CLIFF PALACE. Some look tired, and some look bored, but most are listening as the ranger explains the rules and regulations for their trip into Cliff Palace. It had been a longtime since visitors wore suits to the park!

CULTURE AT MESA VERDE. A Telluride string quartet brings a moment of culture and quiet to Mesa Verde and to the tourists' day. Special weekends, such as ones devoted to native crafts, also attracted visitors.

BEN CAMPBELL. U.S. Congressional representative Ben Campbell speaks at the June 13, 1987, opening of Badger House. The National Park Service was continually trying to spread the increasing numbers of visitors around the park.

BADGER HOUSE. Ben Campbell (second from right), Supt. Robert Hyder (second from left), national park officials, and Mesa Verde staff join to hold and cut the ribbon officially opening Badger House.

HILLARY CLINTON. First Lady Hillary Clinton speaks on behalf of the "Save America's Treasures" national program in May 1999. Over the years, Mesa Verde has welcomed many national leaders and distinguished archaeologists.

PHOTO OP WITH HILLARY. On a beautiful May day, the entire park staff and a few others have their picture taken with Hillary Clinton. Her visit also called attention to the park and its needs.

SODA CANYON. To examine or stabilize some of the isolated cliff sites takes a good deal of skill and a dash of courage for the park staff and other workers. Here a worker is going down the side of Soda Canyon.

MAINTENANCE. Park buildings and the prehistoric structures are constantly in need of repair and/or stabilization. In cases like this, here at Spruce Tree House, it gives the tourist a firsthand view of the park maintenance and their tax money at work.

LIGHTNING FIRES. Mesa Verde ranks second in the United States of places most hit by lightning. Consequently, fires have always been a threat and danger. This 1996 fire closed the park and ushered in a particularly fire-racked few years.

Worst Modern Fire. Perhaps the worst modern fire occurred in June 2002. It not only closed the park, but also left a darkened remembrance for all visitors to see and ponder as they drove out to Chapin Mesa. It will be decades before the trees return. (Courtesy of the author.)

Fire's Charred Remains. This charred sign shows how close the fires came to some of the historic structures. Long House and the other sites on Wetherill Mesa have still not become as popular as those on Chapin Mesa.

FIRE'S AFTERMATH. A visit to Mesa Verde in the winter is a different experience. Right after the 21st-century fires, it gave the appearance of desolation. (Courtesy of the author.)

CHILDREN AT MESA VERDE. Mesa Verde can be a fascinating place for children, particularly if an enthusiastic ranger takes time out to explain some of the wonders and mysteries of this fascinating park.

MORE CHILDREN. Sometimes, despite the best efforts of a ranger, a young visitor may be bored. Hopefully "seeds" were planted, and he will remember a little bit about this park and some of its mysteries.

MAINTENANCE. It requires constant checking and maintenance to stabilize the park sites. It can be both an adventure and dangerous, as this worker demonstrates. It is also exasperating because there are never enough funds to maintain sites properly.

ON GUARD. Crews and individuals are regularly on guard throughout the park. In the 21st century, the threats are many, and the dwellings are older and more fragile.

Far View Saved. It would seem that the Far View Visitor Center was about to be engulfed in flames, but it was not. In all the major fires, fire crews from throughout the region came to the park.

Deer. Among the variety of sights in the park are mule deer and other wild animals. Indeed, during hunting season, the park provides a refuge, as some frustrated hunters find out.

WILD ANIMALS. Seeing wild animals in the park is quite a thrill, but they are not household pets. Meeting a bear, mountain lion, or even a skunk can be exciting at best but also an unpleasant experience if a visitor treats them in a familiar manner. (Courtesy of John Ninnemann.)

CAMPERS. Campers must be parked near the entrance, even for those planning on just a short visit in the park. The roads inside the park are narrow and, on peak season days, crowded, as they were in all the following photographs taken in 2008. (Courtesy of John Ninnemann.)

ADMISSION. Tickets need to be purchased now to visit Cliff Palace and Balcony House at a specified time. The sign on the wall warns visitors: "Visiting the Cliff dwelling will involve Strenuous Hiking & Climbing." (Courtesy of John Ninnemann.)

CHALLENGES. Where to go in the park depends on how much time one has and one's physical condition. The elevation within the park is higher than many people suspect. It is up to the tourist to decide what challenges they want. (Courtesy of John Ninnemann.)

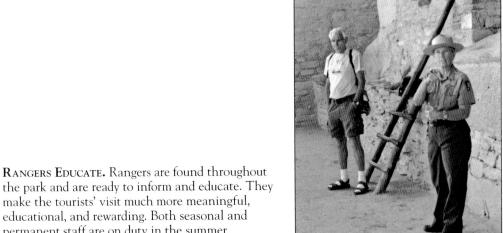

RANGERS EDUCATE. Rangers are found throughout the park and are ready to inform and educate. They make the tourists' visit much more meaningful, educational, and rewarding. Both seasonal and permanent staff are on duty in the summer months. (Courtesy of John Ninnemann.)

ADVENTURE. There is nothing like an adventure on vacation. Climbing into a kiva gives one the feeling of prehistoric times and is less scary than climbing out of Balcony House. (Courtesy of John Ninnemann.)

Automobiles in Summer. On crowded summer days, Mesa Verde's parking lots are full from Chapin Mesa to the rim views to Wetherill Mesa. Knife Edge Road may be gone, but some drivers still do not enjoy driving into the park.

Animals at Night. Driving in the park at dusk or after dark can be a harrowing experience for those who do not take care. Animals of all sizes come out to feed, and highway curves limit a driver's vision. (Courtesy of John Ninnemann.)

BILINGUAL RANGERS. One of the ongoing problems now that Mesa Verde is a World Heritage Cultural Site is finding bilingual rangers. This French couple is obviously happy to discover someone who can speak their language. (Courtesy of John Ninnemann.)

BALCONY HOUSE. It is no easier getting out of Balcony House in 2008 than it was a generation or so ago. Now, however, visitors are forewarned clearly about the adventure they are about to undertake.

TOURISTS IN SUMMER. On a summer day, a steady stream of visitors walks through Spruce Tree and Cliff Palace. On hot days, the climbs in and out can be a trying experience for flatlanders. (Courtesy of John Ninnemann.)

TOURING THE SITES. Not every thing to see is found in one of the major sites. Stopping at one of the viewing points allows time to see a variety of canyon sites and enjoy the beauty of this national park. (Courtesy of John Ninnemann.)

PARK RANGERS. Over the decades, the heart and soul of a visit to Mesa Verde has been the National Park Service people. From the rangers at the sites to the staff at headquarters, they have helped, preserved, and informed. (Courtesy of John Ninnemann.)

MYSTERIOUS MESA VERDE. Mesa Verde has always been a mysterious place. It is a Sherlock Holmes mystery for archaeologists and visitors who first arrived over a century ago. Perhaps we will never know all the answers.

VISIT MESA VERDE. Now, dear reader, having read about and seen much of the park's history, it is time to plan a trip to Mesa Verde and savor it for yourself. It is well worth the trip for the entire family. (Courtesy of John Ninnemann.)

DISCOVER THOUSANDS OF LOCAL HISTORY BOOKS
FEATURING MILLIONS OF VINTAGE IMAGES

Arcadia Publishing, the leading local history publisher in the United States, is committed to making history accessible and meaningful through publishing books that celebrate and preserve the heritage of America's people and places.

Find more books like this at
www.arcadiapublishing.com

Search for your hometown history, your old stomping grounds, and even your favorite sports team.

Consistent with our mission to preserve history on a local level, this book was printed in South Carolina on American-made paper and manufactured entirely in the United States. Products carrying the accredited Forest Stewardship Council (FSC) label are printed on 100 percent FSC-certified paper.

MADE IN THE  USA